MERRY CHRIST

THANK YOU SO MUCH FOR BUYING MY BOOK! BEFORE STARTING PLAYING, PLEASE READ:

HOW TO PLAY?

1 DIVIDE INTO TEAMS OR PLAY SOLO. DECIDE WHO WILL READ THE QUESTIONS FIRST AND GRAB A PEN TO KEEP TRACK OF EVERYONE'S SCORE.

2 EACH PLAYER OR TEAM TAKES TURNS ANSWERING TRIVIA QUESTIONS. CHOOSE FROM EASY, MEDIUM, OR HARD QUESTIONS TO LEVEL UP THE FUN!

3 AT THE END OF THE GAME, TALLY UP THE SCORES. THE TEAM OR PLAYER WITH THE HIGHEST SCORE EARNS THE TITLE OF CHRISTMAS TRIVIA CHAMPION!

ENJOY THE SPECIAL GIFT INSIDE

https://bit.ly/*********

THE GIFT IN PAGE 9

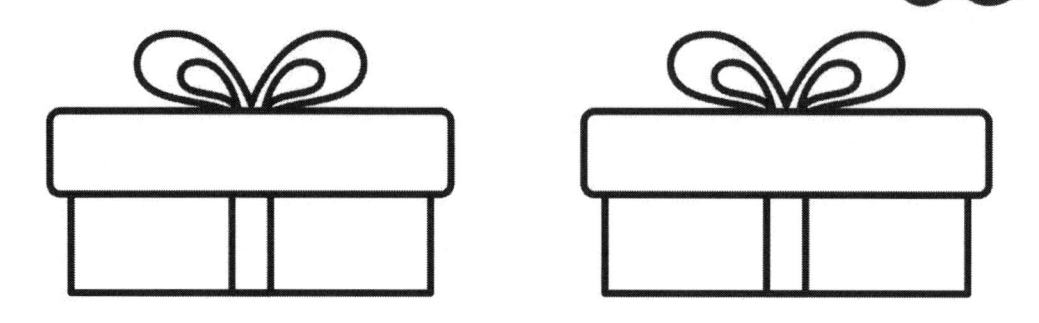

COPYRIGHT © 2025

ALL RIGHTS RESERVED. NO PART OF THIS PUBLICATION MAY BE REPRODUCED, DISTRIBUTED, OR TRANSMITTED IN ANY FORM OR BY ANY MEANS, INCLUDING PHOTOCOPYING, RECORDING, OR OTHER ELECTRONIC OR MECHANICAL METHODS, WITHOUT THE PRIOR WRITTEN PERMISSION OF THE PUBLISHER, EXCEPT IN THE CASE OF BRIEF QUOTATIONS EMBODIED IN CRITICAL REVIEWS AND CERTAIN OTHER NONCOMMERCIAL USES PERMITTED BY COPYRIGHT LAW.

THIS BOOK BELONGS TO:

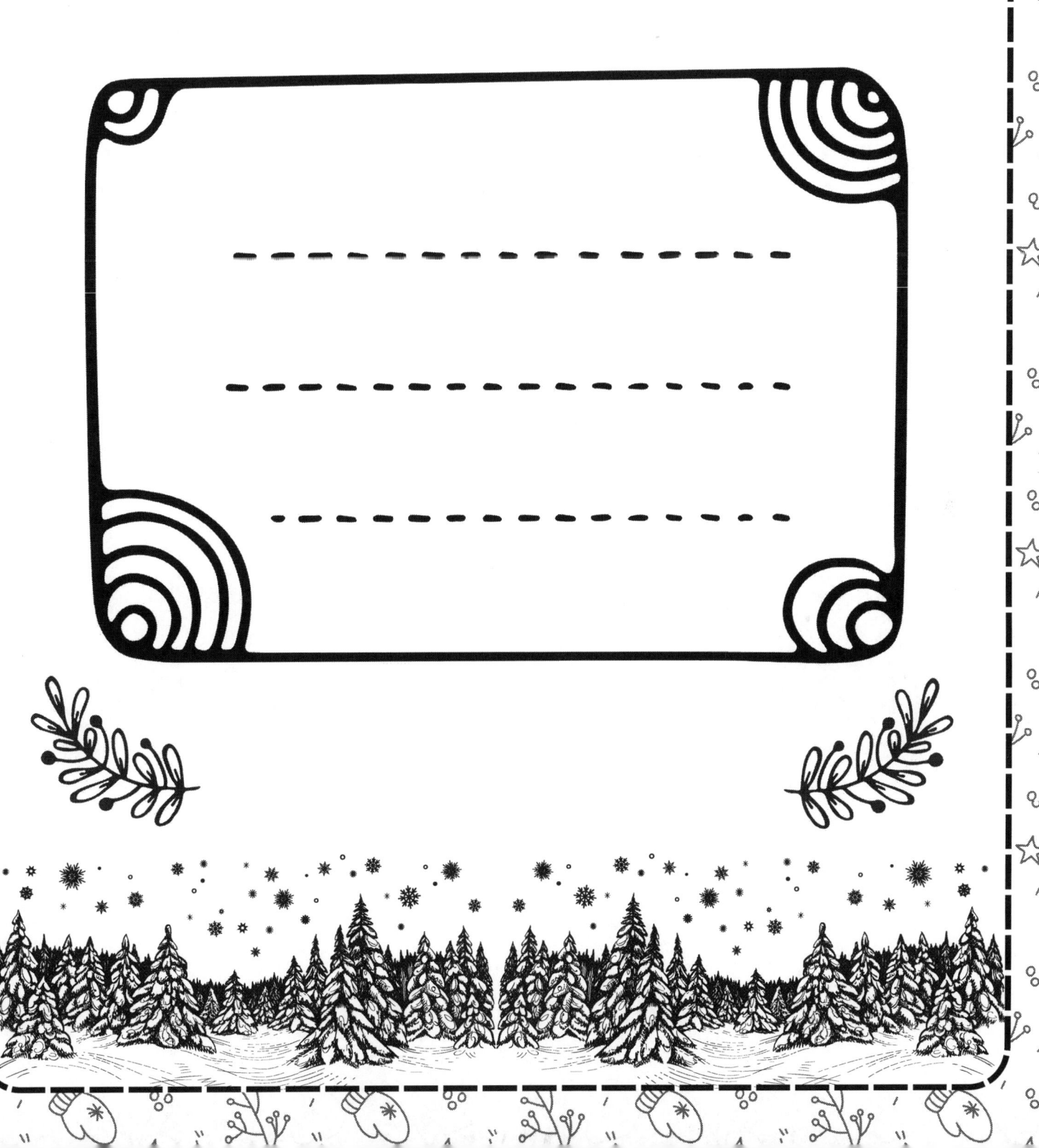

QUIZ - 1

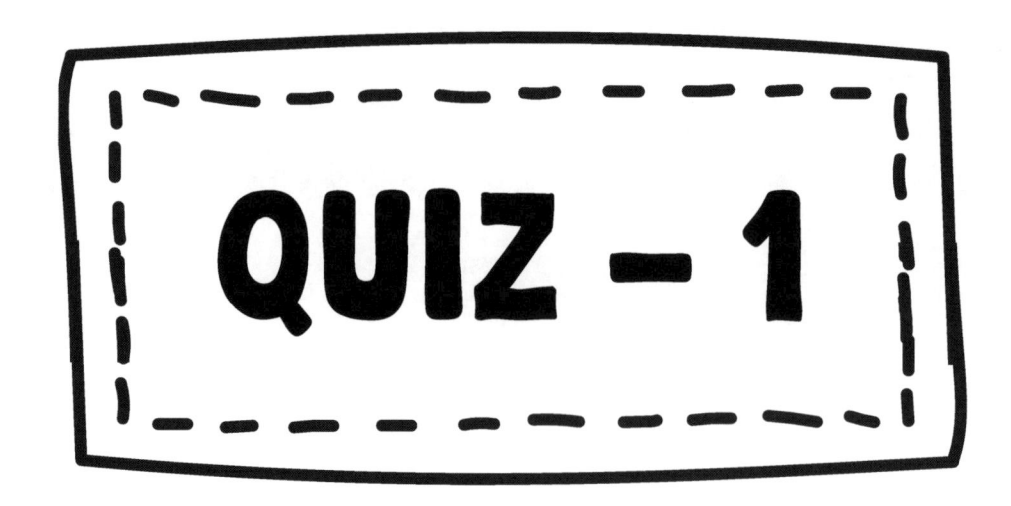

WHAT FAMOUS CHRISTMAS SONG WAS ORIGINALLY IN THE MOVIE "MEET ME IN ST. LOUIS"?

❄❄*❄*❄*❄*

HAVE YOURSELF A MERRY LITTLE CHRISTMAS

QUIZ - 2

WHAT ARE THE TWO MOST POPULAR ITEMS TO PLACE ON THE TOP OF A CHRISTMAS TREE?

❄❄*❄*❄*❄*❄*

STAR AND ANGEL

QUIZ - 3

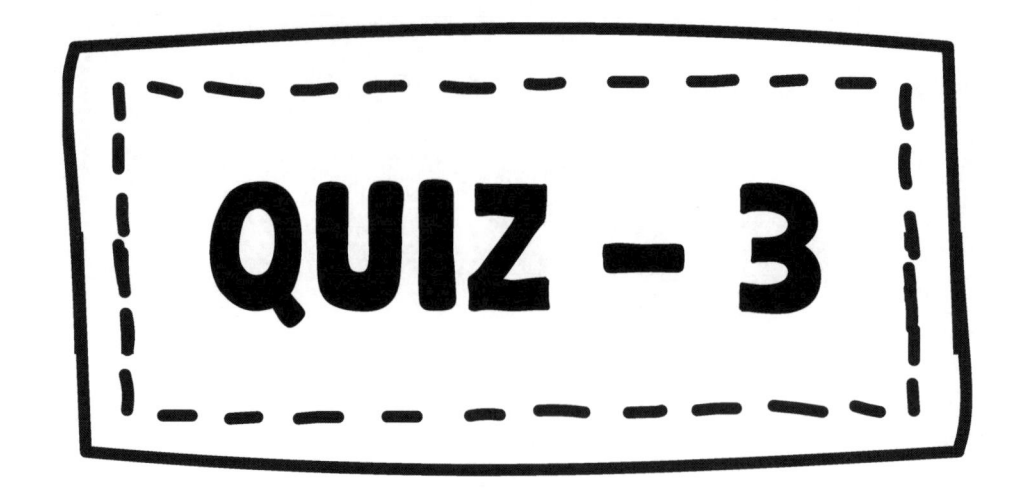

WHAT IS TRADITIONALLY EATEN FOR DESSERT AT CHRISTMAS IN AUSTRALIA?

✻❋✻❋✻❋✻❋✻❋✻

PAVLOVA

QUIZ - 4

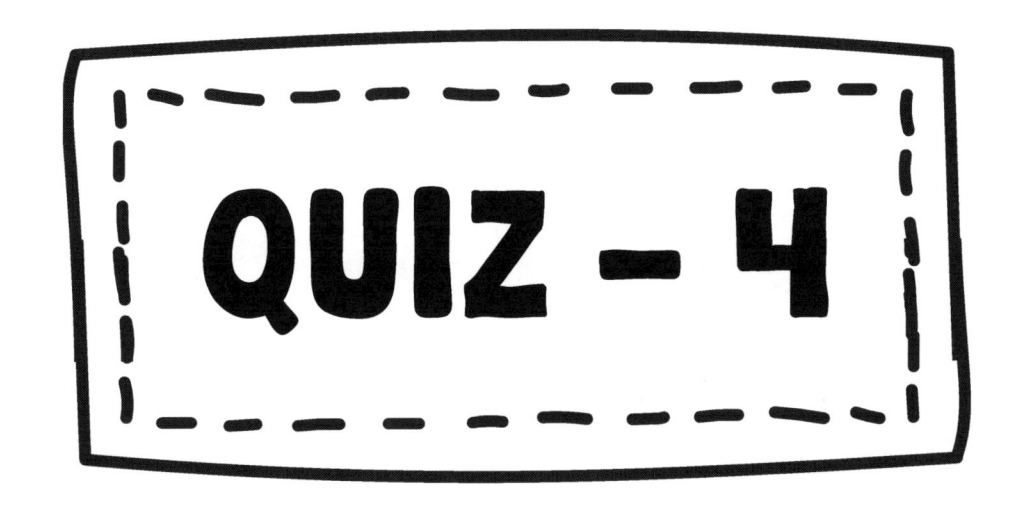

WHAT FRUIT IS MENTIONED IN THE SONG "THE TWELVE DAYS OF CHRISTMAS"?

✳❄✳❄✳❄✳❄✳❄✳

A PEAR (FROM "A PARTRIDGE IN A PEAR TREE")

QUIZ - 5

WHAT IS SANTA CLAUS CALLED IN FINLAND?

❄❄*❄*❄*❄*

JOULUPUK KI

HO-HO-HO!!

HERE IS YOUR GIFT

https://bit.ly/4eACVxP

TAP THIS LINK IN THE BROWSER AND ENJOY! IF YOU LOVED THE BOOK AND THE IDEA GIVE US

★★★★★

QUIZ - 6

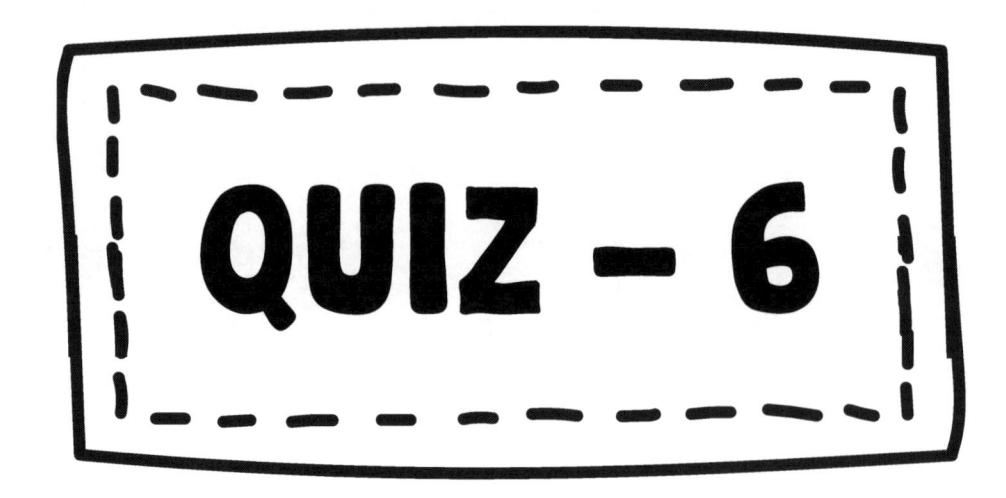

IN THE MOVIE "ELF" WHAT IS THE FIRST RULE OF THE CODE OF ELVES?

❄❄*❄*❄*❄*

TREAT EVERY DAY LIKE CHRISTMAS

QUIZ - 7

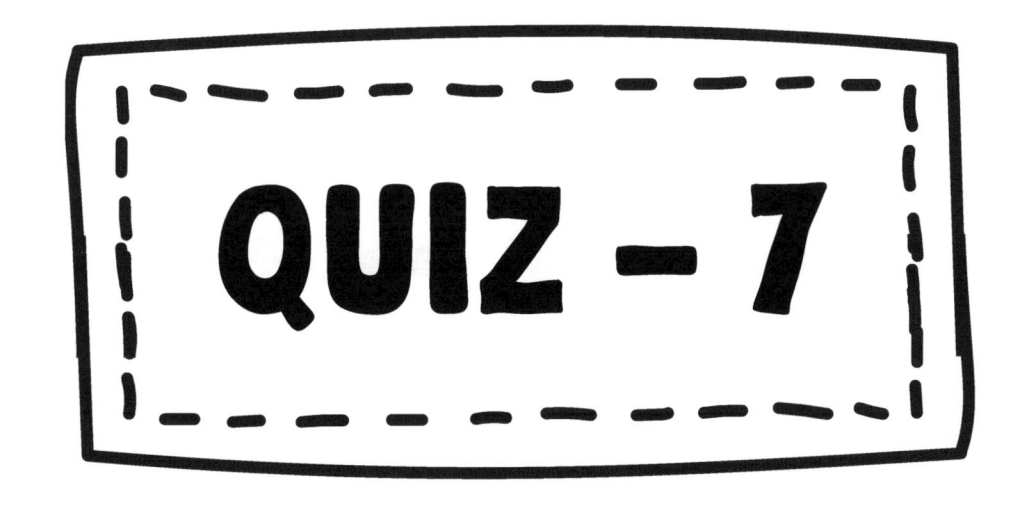

WHAT WAS FROSTY THE SNOWMAN'S NOSE MADE OF?

✻❋✻❋✻❋✻❋✻❋✻

A BUTTON

QUIZ - 8

IN WHICH COUNTRY DID THE TRADITION OF PUTTING UP A CHRISTMAS TREE ORIGINATE?

❄❄❄❄❄

GERMANY

QUIZ - 9

WHAT IS THE NAME OF THE ANIMATED CHRISTMAS TV SPECIAL THAT FEATURES A MAGICAL HAT BRINGING A SNOWMAN TO LIFE?

❄❄*❄*❄*❄*❄*

FROSTY THE SNOWMAN

QUIZ - 10

WHAT CHRISTMAS SONG HAS THE LYRICS "OH, BRING US SOME FIGGY PUDDING"?

❄ ❄ ❄ ❄ ❄

"WE WISH YOU A MERRY CHRISTMAS"

QUIZ - 11

IN "A CHRISTMAS STORY", WHAT WAS THE NAME OF THE DEPARTMENT STORE WHERE RALPHIE SEES THE RED RYDER BB GUN?

✶❋✶❋✶❋✶❋✶❋✶

HIGBEE'S

QUIZ - 12

IN THE SONG "JINGLE BELLS," WHAT KIND OF SLEIGH IS MENTIONED?

❄❄❄❄❄❄

A ONE-HORSE OPEN SLEIGH

QUIZ - 13

WHAT IS THE NAME OF THE MAIN VILLAIN IN "THE NIGHTMARE BEFORE CHRISTMAS"?

❋❋*❋*❋*❋*❋*

OOGIE BOOGIE

QUIZ - 14

WHAT FAMOUS CHRISTMAS CAROL WAS SUNG BY SOLDIERS DURING THE 1914 CHRISTMAS TRUCE?

❄❄*❄*❄*❄*

"SILENT NIGHT"

QUIZ - 15

IN "HOME ALONE" WHERE IS THE MCCALLISTER FAMILY GOING ON VACATION WHEN THEY LEAVE KEVIN BEHIND?

❄❄*❄*❄*❄*❄*

PARIS

QUIZ - 16

WHAT IS RALPHIE'S LITTLE BROTHER'S NAME IN "A CHRISTMAS STORY"?

❄❄*❄*❄*❄*

RANDY

QUIZ - 17

IN "IT'S A WONDERFUL LIFE", WHAT IS THE NAME OF GEORGE BAILEY'S GUARDIAN ANGEL?

❋❋*❋*❋*❋*❋*

CLARENCE ODBODY

QUIZ - 18

WHO PLAYED THE GRINCH IN THE 2000 LIVE-ACTION VERSION OF "HOW THE GRINCH STOLE CHRISTMAS"?

❄❄❄❄❄

JIM CARREY

QUIZ - 19

WHAT IS THE NAME OF THE BOY LEFT BEHIND IN THE TRAIN STATION IN "THE POLAR EXPRESS"?

❄❄*❄*❄*❄*

BILLY

QUIZ - 20

IN "HOME ALONE 2", WHICH CITY DOES KEVIN MISTAKENLY GET SENT TO?

✳❄✳❄✳❄✳❄✳❄✳

NEW YORK CITY

QUIZ - 21

WHO ORIGINALLY SANG "WHITE CHRISTMAS"?

❄❄*❄*❄*❄*❄*

BING CROSBY

QUIZ - 22

IN "JINGLE BELL ROCK", WHAT TIME IS IT MENTIONED AS BEING THE BEST TIME TO ROCK THE NIGHT AWAY?

❄❄❄❄❄❄❄

THE JINGLE BELL TIME

QUIZ - 23

WHAT DO PEOPLE TRADITIONALLY PUT ON TOP OF A CHRISTMAS TREE?

A STAR OR AN ANGEL

QUIZ - 24

WHAT IS THE OPENING LINE OF "IT'S THE MOST WONDERFUL TIME OF THE YEAR"?

✳❄✳❄✳❄✳❄✳❄✳

IT'S THE MOST WONDERFUL TIME OF THE YEAR!"

QUIZ - 25

WHAT DID MY TRUE LOVE GAVE TO ME ON THE 7TH DAY OF CHRISTMAS IN THE SONG "THE TWELVE DAYS OF CHRISTMAS"?

SEVEN SWANS A SWIMMING

QUIZ - 26

WHAT SONG IS SUNG BY THE CHILDREN IN THE PEANUTS CHRISTMAS SPECIAL?

✳❄✳❄✳❄✳❄✳❄✳

"CHRISTMAS TIME IS HERE" ND "HARK, THE HERALD ANGELS SING"

QUIZ - 27

WHO WROTE THE SONG "JINGLE BELLS"?

❄❄*❄*❄*❄*❄*

JAMES LORD PIERPONT

QUIZ - 28

WHAT POPULAR CHRISTMAS CAROL WAS ORIGINALLY WRITTEN FOR THANKSGIVING?

*❄***❄***❄***❄***❄**

JINGLE BELLS

QUIZ - 29

IN THE SONG "FROSTY THE SNOWMAN", WHAT MADE FROSTY COME TO LIFE?

❄❄*❄*❄*❄*

AN OLD SILK HAT

QUIZ - 30

WHO SINGS "ALL I WANT FOR WHO SINGS "ALL I WANT FOR CHRISTMAS IS YOU"?

❄❄❄❄❄

MARIAH CAREY

QUIZ - 31

WHAT IS SANTA'S REAL NAME IN THE SANTA CLAUSE MOVIE SERIES?

❄❄❄❄❄❄

SCOTT CALVIN

QUIZ - 32

WHAT ARE THE NAMES OF SANTA'S REINDEER?

❄❄*❄*❄*❄*❄*

DASHER, DANCER, PRANCER, VIXEN, COMET, UPID, DONNER, BLITZEN, AND RUDOLPH

QUIZ - 33

WHERE DOES SANTA CLAUS LIVE?

❄❄*❄*❄*❄*

THE NORTH POLE

QUIZ - 34

WHICH COUNTRY IS CREDITED WITH CREATING EGGNOG?

✳❄✳❄✳❄✳❄✳❄✳

ENGLAND

QUIZ - 35

WHAT SNACK IS TRADITIONALLY LEFT OUT FOR SANTA?

❋❋*❋*❋*❋*❋*

MILK AND COOKIES

QUIZ - 36

WHO HELPS SANTA MAKE TOYS IN HIS WORKSHOP?

❄❄*❄*❄*❄*❄*

ELVES

QUIZ - 37

WHAT IS SANTA'S WIFE'S NAME?

❋❋❋❋❋❋

MRS. CLAUS

QUIZ - 38

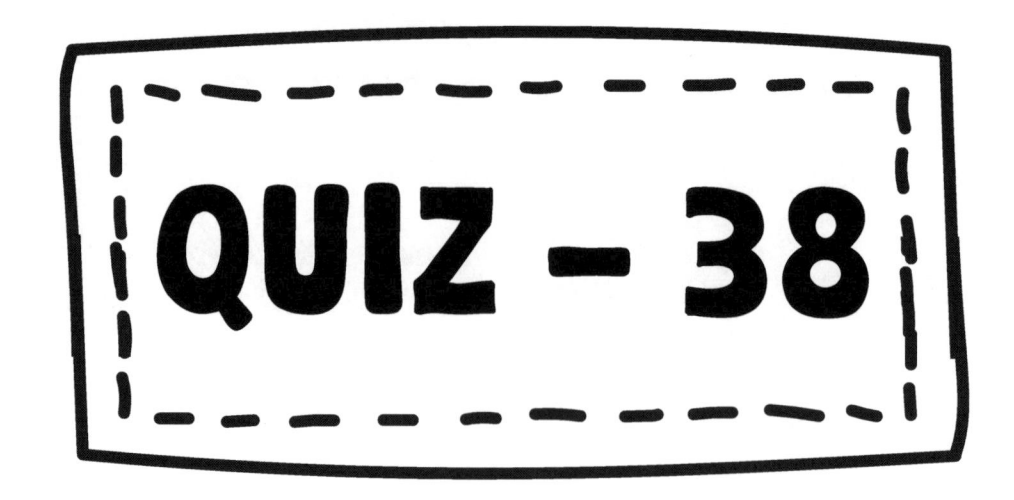

HOW DOES SANTA ENTER PEOPLE'S HOMES ON CHRISTMAS EVE?

✳❄✳❄✳❄✳❄✳❄✳

CHRISTMAS EVE?

QUIZ - 39

WHAT DO YOU TRADITIONALLY LEAVE FOR SANTA'S REINDEER?

❄❄*❄*❄*❄*❄*

CARROTS

QUIZ - 40

WHAT IS THE NAME OF SANTA'S REINDEER WITH A GLOWING RED NOSE?

❄❄*❄*❄*❄*❄*

RUDOLPH

QUIZ - 41

IN WHICH COUNTRY IS SANTA CLAUS KNOWN AS PÈRE NOËL?

❋❋❋❋❋❋❋❋❋❋

FRANCE

QUIZ - 42

WHAT IS THE TRADITIONAL DRINK SERVED DURING CHRISTMAS IN THE UK CALLED?

MULLED WINE

QUIZ - 43

WHAT KIND OF PIE IS A TRADITIONAL CHRISTMAS DESSERT IN THE UK?

❋❋*❋*❋*❋*❋*

MINCE PIE

QUIZ - 44

WHAT IS THE MOST POPULAR CHRISTMAS DINNER MEAT IN THE UNITED STATES?

✳❄✳❄✳❄✳❄✳❄✳

TURKEY

QUIZ - 45

WHAT PLANT IS TRADITIONALLY HUNG OVER DOORWAYS DURING CHRISTMAS TO ENCOURAGE KISSING?

❄❄*❄*❄*❄*

MISTLETOE

QUIZ - 46

WHAT IS FIGGY PUDDING MADE FROM?

✳❄✳❄✳❄✳❄✳❄✳

DRIED FRUITS AND SPICES

QUIZ - 47

WHICH DRINK IS KNOWN AS "MILK PUNCH"?

❄❄*❄*❄*❄*❄*

EGGNOG

QUIZ - 48

IN THE SONG "WE WISH YOU A MERRY CHRISTMAS" WHAT IS DEMANDED?

✳❄✳❄✳❄✳❄✳❄✳

FIGGY PUDDING

QUIZ - 49

WHAT IS TRADITIONALLY HIDDEN INSIDE A CHRISTMAS PUDDING?

A COIN

QUIZ - 50

WHAT'S THE NAME OF THE FRENCH CHRISTMAS DESSERT SHAPED LIKE A LOG?

❄❄❄❄❄

BÛCHE DE NOËL

QUIZ - 51

WHAT IS THE MAIN INGREDIENT IN GINGERBREAD COOKIES?

❄❄*❄*❄*❄*❄*

GINGER

QUIZ - 52

WHAT FRUIT IS USED TO DECORATE A TRADITIONAL CHRISTMAS HAM?

❄❄❄❄❄❄

PINEAPPLE

QUIZ - 53

WHAT IS ANOTHER NAME FOR CHRISTMAS EVE?

❄❄*❄*❄*❄*

HOLY NIGHT

QUIZ - 54

IN THE BIBLE, WHERE WAS JESUS BORN?

BETHLEHEM

QUIZ - 55

WHAT WAS THE NAME OF JESUS' MOTHER?

❄❄❄❄❄❄

MARY

QUIZ - 56

When is St. Nicholas Day celebrated in most European countries?

❄❄❄❄❄❄

December 6th

QUIZ - 57

WHO WERE THE FIRST TO VISIT JESUS IN THE MANGER?

❋❄❋❄❋❄❋❄❋❄❋

THE SHEPHERDS

QUIZ - 58

WHAT GIFT DID THE WISE MEN BRING TO JESUS?

✳❄✳❄✳❄✳❄✳❄✳

GOLD, FRANKINCENSE, AND MYRRH

QUIZ - 59

WHAT ANGEL VISITED MARY TO TELL HER SHE WOULD GIVE BIRTH TO JESUS?

❄❄*❄*❄*❄*

GABRIEL

QUIZ - 60

WHO WAS THE ROMAN EMPEROR AT THE TIME OF JESUS' BIRTH?

❋❋*❋*❋*❋*

CAESAR AUGUSTUS

QUIZ - 61

WHICH ANIMALS ARE TRADITIONALLY DEPICTED IN THE NATIVITY SCENE?

❄❄❄❄❄

SHEEP, DONKEYS, OXEN

QUIZ - 62

WHAT TOWN DID MARY AND JOSEPH TRAVEL FROM BEFORE JESUS WAS BORN?

❄❄*❄*❄*❄*❄*

NAZARETH

QUIZ - 63

WHAT IS THE MEANING OF THE NAME EMMANUEL?

❄ ❄ ❄ ❄ ❄

GOD WITH US

QUIZ - 64

WHICH FAMOUS WRITER PENNED "A CHRISTMAS CAROL"?

❋❋*❋*❋*❋*

CHARLES DICKENS

QUIZ - 65

WHAT YEAR WAS CHRISTMAS DECLARED A FEDERAL HOLIDAY IN THE UNITED STATES?

✳❄✳❄✳❄✳❄✳❄✳

1870

QUIZ - 65

WHO STARTED THE CHRISTMAS TRADITION OF SENDING CHRISTMAS CARDS?

❄❄*❄*❄*❄*

SIR HENRY COLE

QUIZ - 66

WHICH OCEAN IS CHRISTMAS ISLAND LOCATED IN?

❄❄*❄*❄*❄*

INDIAN OCEAN

QUIZ - 67

WHICH COUNTRY CELEBRATES THE FEAST OF THE 7 FISHES ON CHRISTMAS EVE?

❄❄*❄*❄*❄*

ITALY

QUIZ - 69

WHEN WAS THE FIRST CHRISTMAS CARD SENT?

✳❄✳❄✳❄✳❄✳❄✳

1843

QUIZ - 70

WHAT DOES THE NAME "CHRISTMAS" MEAN?

✳❄✳❄✳❄✳❄✳❄✳

CHRIST'S MASS

QUIZ - 71

WHAT EVENT DOES ADVENT COUNTDOWN TO?

❄❄❄❄❄❄

THE BIRTH OF JESUS (CHRISTMAS)

QUIZ - 72

WHAT 16TH CENTURY REFORMER HELPED POPULARIZE THE TRADITION OF CHRISTMAS TREES?

❋❋❋❋❋❋

MARTIN LUTHER

QUIZ - 73

WHAT ANCIENT ROMAN FESTIVAL WAS CELEBRATED AT THE SAME TIME AS CHRISTMAS?

SATURNALIA

QUIZ - 74

IN THE UK, WHAT IS A CHRISTMAS CRACKER?

✳❄✳❄✳❄✳❄✳❄✳

A FESTIVE TABLE DECORATION THAT MAKES A POPPING SOUND WHEN PULLED APART

QUIZ - 75

IN WHICH COUNTRY IS "FELIZ NAVIDAD" A COMMON CHRISTMAS GREETING?

❄❄*❄*❄*❄*

SPAIN

QUIZ - 76

WHAT DO AUSTRALIANS OFTEN DO ON CHRISTMAS DAY?

✳❋✳❋✳❋✳❋✳❋✳

HAVE A BARBECUE OR GO TO THE BEACH

QUIZ - 77

WHICH COUNTRY CELEBRATES "LA BEFANA," WHERE AN OLD WOMAN DELIVERS GIFTS ON JANUARY 6TH?

❋❋❋❋❋❋❋❋❋❋❋

ITALY

QUIZ - 78

WHAT DO THE SWEDISH CALL SANTA CLAUS?

❄❄*❄*❄*❄*

JULTOMTE OR TOMTE

QUIZ - 79

IN WHICH COUNTRY DO THEY EAT TAMALES ON CHRISTMAS?

❄❄❄❄❄

MEXICO

QUIZ - 80

WHAT DO PEOPLE IN ICELAND TRADITIONALLY EXCHANGE ON CHRISTMAS EVE?

✳❄✳❄✳❄✳❄✳❄✳

BOOKS

QUIZ - 81

WHAT DO CHRISTMAS CRACKERS CONTAIN?

❄❄*❄*❄*❄*

A PAPER CROWN, A SMALL TOY, AND A JOKE

QUIZ - 82

WHAT IS SANTA CLAUS CALLED IN ITALY?

❄❄*❄*❄*❄*

BABBO NATALE

QUIZ - 83

IN WHICH COUNTRY DO CHILDREN LEAVE OUT SHOES FOR SANTA INSTEAD OF STOCKINGS?

❄❄*❄*❄*❄*❄*

THE NETHERLANDS

QUIZ - 84

WHAT CHRISTMAS TRADITION IS OBSERVED IN THE PHILIPPINES WITH THE "SIMBANG GABI"?

A SERIES OF NINE DAWN MASSES LEADING UP TO CHRISTMAS

QUIZ - 85

IN WHICH EUROPEAN COUNTRY DO CHILDREN RECEIVE PRESENTS FROM ST. BASIL ON NEW YEAR'S DAY?

❋❋❋❋❋❋❋❋❋❋❋

GREECE

QUIZ - 86

WHAT DO CHILDREN IN GERMANY RECEIVE FOR CHRISTMAS ON DECEMBER 6TH?

❋❋❋❋❋❋❋❋❋❋❋

GIFTS FROM ST. NICHOLAS

QUIZ - 87

WHAT IS THE CHRISTMAS EVE TRADITION IN NORWAY OF HIDING?

BROOMS (TO AVOID WITCHES STEALING THEM)

QUIZ - 88

WHAT FAMOUS CHRISTMAS TALE BEGINS WITH "MARLEY WAS DEAD: TO BEGIN WITH"?

✳❄✳❄✳❄✳❄✳❄✳

A CHRISTMAS CAROL

QUIZ - 89

IN JAPAN, WHAT FAST-FOOD CHAIN IS CONSIDERED A CHRISTMAS TRADITION?

❄❄*❄*❄*❄*❄*

KFC

QUIZ - 90

Who wrote "The Nutcracker and the Mouse King", the story that inspired the Nutcracker Ballet?

E.T.A. Hoffmann

QUIZ - 91

IN "HOW THE GRINCH STOLE CHRISTMAS", WHAT IS THE NAME OF THE GRINCH'S DOG?

❄ ❄ ❄ ❄ ❄ ❄

MAX

QUIZ - 92

WHAT IS THE NAME OF THE MAIN CHARACTER IN "THE POLAR EXPRESS" BOOK?

※※※※※※※※※※※

HE IS UNNAMED

QUIZ - 93

IN "TWAS THE NIGHT BEFORE CHRISTMAS", WHAT CREATURE WAS "NOT STIRRING"?

❄❄*❄*❄*❄*

A MOUSE

QUIZ - 94

IN "THE LION, THE WITCH AND THE WARDROBE", WHICH CHARACTER REPRESENTS FATHER CHRISTMAS?

❄❄*❄*❄*❄*

FATHER CHRISTMAS

QUIZ - 95

WHAT WAS THE FIRST GIFT OF CHRISTMAS IN "THE POLAR EXPRESS"?

✶❄✶❄✶❄✶❄✶❄✶

A BELL FROM SANTA'S SLEIGH

QUIZ - 96

WHO IS THE MAIN GIRL IN "THE NUTCRACKER"?

✳❄✳❄✳❄✳❄✳❄✳

A GERMAN GIRL NAMED CLARA STAHLBAUM

QUIZ - 97

WHO WAS THE AUTHOR OF THE POEM "A VISIT FROM ST. NICHOLAS"?

❄❄❄❄❄❄

CLEMENT CLARKE MOORE

QUIZ - 98

IN "A CHRISTMAS CAROL", WHAT IS SCROOGE'S FAMOUS CATCH PHRASE?

❄❄*❄*❄*❄*

"BAH, HUMBUG!"

QUIZ - 99

WHAT ARE CANDY CANES SHAPED LIKE?

A SHEPHERD'S CROOK

QUIZ - 100

WHAT FRUIT IS TRADITIONALLY PUT IN CHRISTMAS STOCKINGS?

✳❄✳❄✳❄✳❄✳❄✳

AN ORANGE

QUIZ - 101

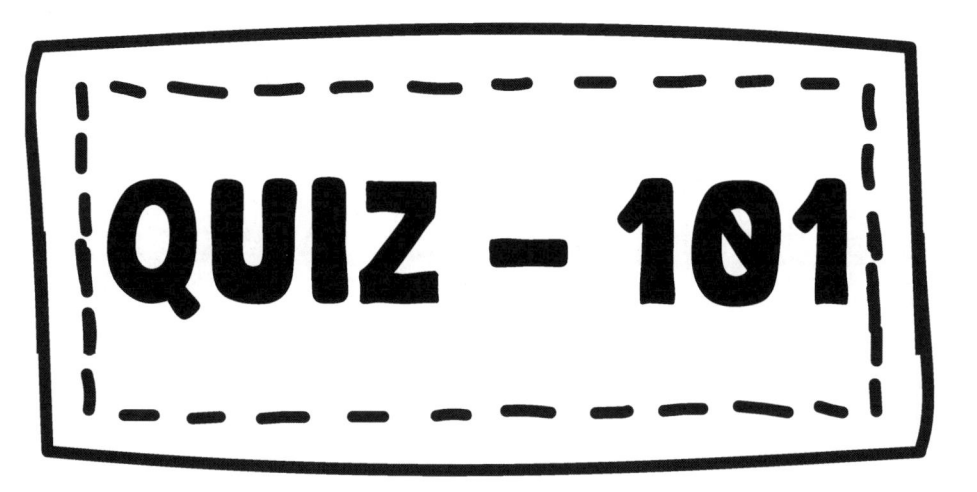

IN THE CLASSIC CHRISTMAS STORY, HOW MANY GHOSTS VISIT EBENEZER SCROOGE?

✻❋✻❋✻❋✻❋✻❋✻

FOUR (INCLUDING JACOB MARLEY)

QUIZ - 102

WHAT CHRISTMAS SONG HOLDS THE RECORD FOR THE MOST SALES OF ALL TIME?

❄❄*❄*❄*❄*

WHITE CHRISTMAS BY BING CROSBY

QUIZ - 103

WHAT TRADITIONAL CHRISTMAS DECORATION IS ACTUALLY A PARASITIC PLANT?

※❄※❄※❄※❄※❄※

MISTLETOE

QUIZ - 104

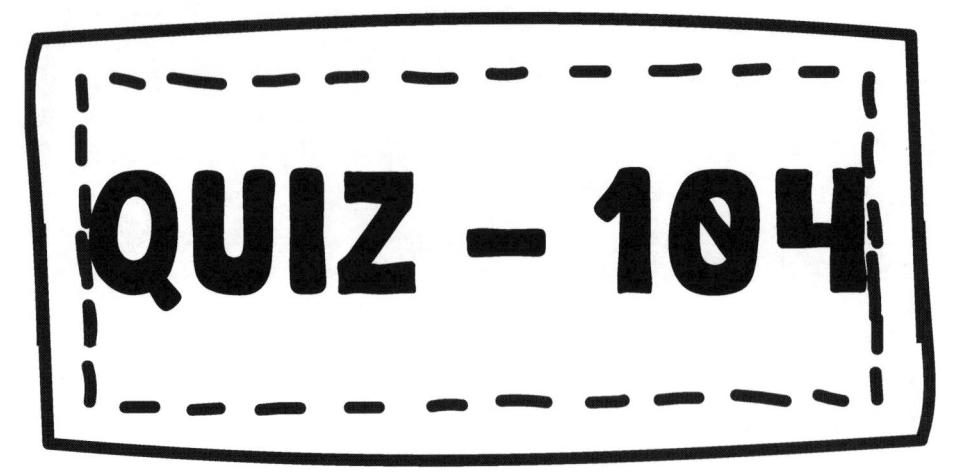

WHAT IS THE MOST POPULAR CHRISTMAS MOVIE OF ALL TIME?

❄❄*❄*❄*❄*

HOME ALONE

QUIZ - 105

HOW MANY REINDEER DOES SANTA HAVE INCLUDING RUDOLPH?

❄❄*❄*❄*❄*

NINE

Printed in Great Britain
by Amazon